[illegible]LLY BUDD & TYPEE

[illegible]NOTES

including

- *Life and Background*
- *Introductions to the Novels*
- *Brief Synopses*
- *Lists of Characters*
- *Summaries and Commentaries*
- *Critical Analyses*
- *Review Questions and Essay Topics*
- *Selected Bibliographies*

by
O. B. Emerson, Ph.D.
Department of English
University of Alabama

INCORPORATED
LINCOLN, NEBRASKA 68501

ISBN 0-8220-0238-8

Printed in U.S.A.

1988 Printing

Cliffs Notes, Inc. Lincoln, Nebraska

CONTENTS

MELVILLE'S LIFE AND BACKGROUND 5

GENERAL INTRODUCTION 8

"BILLY BUDD" NOTES

BRIEF SYNOPSIS 10

LIST OF MAIN CHARACTERS 11

SUMMARIES AND COMMENTARIES 12

Chapters 1-2 13
Chapters 3-5 15
Chapters 6-7 16
Chapters 8-10 17
Chapters 11-14 18
Chapter 15 20
Chapters 16-18 21
Chapter 19 21
Chapter 20 23
Chapters 21-22 24
Chapters 23-24 26
Chapter 25 27
Chapters 26-28 28
Chapters 29-31 29

CRITICAL ANALYSIS 32

Plot 32
Setting 35
Narrative Technique 36
Characters 37
Theme 40
Style 43

REVIEW QUESTIONS AND ESSAY TOPICS 49

SELECTED BIBLIOGRAPHY 51

"TYPEE" NOTES

BRIEF SYNOPSIS 53

CRITICAL ANALYSIS 54

Plot 55
Setting 56
Point of View 57
Characters 58
Theme 60
Style 61

Melville's Life and Background

Born August 1, 1819, in New York City, Herman Melville was the son of Allan and Maria Gansevoort Melville, descendants of English and Dutch colonial families, an ancestry in which he took great pride. Allan Melville died bankrupt in 1832 when Herman was twelve years old. Left destitute with seven other children to rear, Mrs. Melville (who was the prototype of Mrs. Glendinning in *Pierre)* was a cold, imperious, unsympathetic mother, and Melville left home before he was seventeen.

Melville's formal schooling ended when he was fifteen. For a time he tried clerking at a bank in New York City, working in his brother's fur and cap store, farming, and teaching. In 1839 his destiny overtook him when he shipped as a cabin boy on the merchant ship *St. Lawrence* to Liverpool. This voyage, described in detail in *Redburn,* was both romantic and distressing. It instilled in Melville a love for the sea.

Upon his return to this country he again tried teaching, this time at Pittsfield and East Albany. But the sea was in his blood. By 1841 Melville was at sea again, aboard the whaler *Acushnet,* bound from Fairhaven, Massachusetts, for the South Seas. This eighteen-month voyage served as the basis for *Moby Dick.*

The intolerable conditions aboard the ship caused him and a companion, Richard Tobias Greene, to jump ship in the Marquesas. For a month he lived a virtual prisoner among the cannibalistic Typees. His first novel, *Typee,* contains many of his experiences and impressions of his life among the cannibals.

Melville finally escaped on an Australian whaler, from which he deserted at Papeete, in Tahiti. His experiences there are recorded in *Omoo.* Leaving Tahiti he sailed on a whaler to Honolulu, whence he returned to Boston on the frigate *United States.* His life as an ordinary seaman aboard this ship provided him material and inspiration for *White Jacket.* His Harvard and Yale had been the fo'c'sle of a whaling ship, as he later wrote, for he now settled down to writing novels from his experiences in the South Seas.

In 1847 Melville married Elizabeth Shaw, daughter of Lemuel Shaw, chief justice of the commonwealth of Massachusetts. Shaw was an old friend of the Melville family, and Herman dedicated *Typee* to him. Melville and his wife settled in New York, where their first son, Malcolm, was born in 1849. In 1850 the Melvilles moved to "Arrowhead," near Pittsfield, Massachusetts, where Melville was a neighbor of his literary idol, Nathaniel Hawthorne, whom he had met shortly after Melville had contributed an essay on Hawthorne to *Literary World.* Three more children were born: his son Stanwix in 1851, and two daughters, Elizabeth in 1853 and Frances in 1855. Malcolm Melville died in 1867; Stanwix died in 1886.

In 1846 John Murray published *Typee* in England. Famous for publishing only factual books of travel and adventure, Mr. Murray thought he was doing just that, publishing another book of travel and adventure, when he published Melville's first novel.

This work was followed by *Omoo* (1847), *Redburn* (1849), and *White Jacket* (1850). With the publication of these books Melville became enormously popular. Both then and later, as he very much feared, he was known as the man who had lived among the cannibals.

Strange as it may seem to us today his masterpiece, *Moby Dick,* published in 1851, was severely attacked by critics and readers alike and condemned as being uncouth, formless, verbose, and extravagantly emotional.

The publication of *Pierre* in 1852 failed to revive the popular interest Melville had lost after *Moby Dick* was so unfavorably received. In later years several other works were published, including *Israel Potter* (1855), *The Piazza Tales* (1856), *The*

Confidence Man (1857), *Battle Pieces* (1866), *Clarel* (1876), and *John Marr and Other Sailors* (1888).

Melville spent these dark and depressing years traveling, lecturing, and, during 1866-86, serving as inspector of customs at the Port of New York. When Melville died in 1891, the leading literary journal did not know who he was. After much searching and researching around he was remembered by the older generation as the writer who had adventured in the South Seas on a whaler and had lived among the cannibals.

Melville finished *Billy Budd* less than six months before his death in 1891. Suffering a fate similar to that of its neglected and nearly forgotten author, *Billy Budd* was not published until 1924. The appearance of the novel, and of an excellent biography of Melville by Raymond M. Weaver, aroused a revival of interest in Melville's work. His present high reputation dates from 1924.

General Introduction

Since *Typee* and *Billy Budd* are the first and last works of one of America's greatest imaginative authors, it is fitting and proper that they appear together here in a single volume of discussion and commentary. Besides being the alpha and omega of Melville's literary career, they reveal the dichotomy of Melville's nature and express the two themes that appear throughout his writing.

Typee, suggesting a Rousseauistic influence, presents Melville's search for a primitive society which through its isolation could preserve the values civilization has lost. *Billy Budd* may represent a return to Christian verities which, forty years earlier, Melville had embarked on an odyssey to recover.

Ostensibly based on his adventures in the Marquesas, *Typee* is accepted today not as an autobiography or a travel book, but as a romantic novel based to a large extent on fact. In it the reader encounters certain characters and themes which are also present and often more fully developed in Melville's later works. *Typee,* the first great romance of the South Seas, according to Robert Louis Stevenson, stands today as a landmark in the literature of primitive Utopias. *Typee* began Melville's career and brought him popular acclaim and fame as the man who had lived among the cannibals.

On the other hand, when *Billy Budd* finally appeared Melville was little known. Forty-five years had passed between the publication of *Typee* and the completion of *Billy Budd.* Little wonder it appears from a first reading of the two that they have little in common. By comparing and contrasting them we may understand Melville the man and artist a little better, for always the man Melville is present. That his work contains much autobiographical sketching is obvious. But Melville goes beyond that. The autobiographical nature of *Typee* keeps the book from attaining any universal significance. We are reading the adventures of a young man in the South Seas and we very well know it.

In reading *Billy Budd* we are struck by the "Everyman" quality in the title character. All humanity is Billy. The author gives us more than one hint. Billy is twice compared to Adam. His name is not William Budd to us; it is Billy, the familiar. He is the generalized Handsome Sailor, and occasionally the simpler, more universal, "He." Billy is not delineated with a past history to place him in time. He is with us at the age of twenty-one, without a past. The author tells us that he is not a conventional hero and that the story is not a romance. The story is an account of the reality of evil in the life of every man. What happens to Billy happens to all of us. *Typee,* on the other hand, is a romance, an escape. It is, in the final analysis, a refusal that denies life.

Billy Budd, in its acutely painful account of the destruction of good by the forces of evil, is an attempt to deal with life. In the end it is an affirmation of life. "God bless Captain Vere!" Billy says. And Billy is immortalized in art, life's imitation, by the artistry of his ballad-maker friend from the foretop.

Melville's writings, from first to last, were left for a later generation to interpret in almost as many ways as there are readers. Melville, almost completely forgotten from the outbreak of the Civil War until after World War I, is now one of this country's most widely read, frequently discussed, and greatly admired authors. Born in 1819 and dying in 1891, he is historically a nineteenth-century writer. But essentially he is a twentieth-century author, for in this century he has had a rebirth. He belongs here with us.

"Billy Budd" Notes

BRIEF SYNOPSIS

Nearing home after a long voyage, the British merchant ship, the *Rights of Man*, is halted by the H.M.S. *Indomitable*, a man-of-war in need of men. Lieutenant Ratcliffe impresses only one sailor, Billy Budd, who, happy to serve his country, offers no objections. As he leaves he bids farewell by name to the *Rights of Man*.

Aboard the *Indomitable*, Billy is assigned the duties of foretopman. He quickly endears himself to his mates and to the officers under whom he serves, except Claggart, the master-at-arms. The captain of the ship, "Starry" Vere, is a quiet, just, and well-read officer. Claggart, although outwardly placid, is inwardly somewhat mystic and moody. At first he is friendly toward Billy and seems pleased with his performance of duty.

Later Billy is surprised when he is admonished by Claggart's subordinates for petty errors. Fearing punishment, Billy seeks advice from a veteran sailor called the Dansker, who says Jemmy Legs (Claggart) is "down on him." The Dansker's insight proves correct. Squeak, one of Claggart's corporals, sensing the situation, furnishes desired false information to the master-at-arms.

One night while sleeping on deck, Billy is awakened by an afterguardsman who sends him to a secluded spot on the ship. There he asks Billy to join a group of impressed sailors in an insurrection, and offers him money to join the rebellion. Enraged, Billy begins to stutter and threatens to throw the sailor overboard. The sailor flees.

The master-at-arms reports to Captain Vere that Billy is involved in an attempted mutiny. Shocked, the captain orders

Claggart and Billy to come to his cabin. When Claggart faces him with charges of conspiracy, Billy is so dumbfounded that once again he is unable to speak; he can only stammer. To give vent to his feelings, Billy strikes Claggart so forcibly that he kills him.

Captain Vere, in spite of his love for Billy and his knowledge that the act was unintentional, forthwith calls a drum-head court to try the foretopman. England is at war. Recently there have been widespread mutinies in the British fleet. Billy is found guilty. The next morning at sunrise he is hanged from the yardarm. He dies with a blessing on his lips—"God bless Captain Vere!"

While returning to join the Mediterranean fleet, the *Indomitable* encounters the French line-of-battle ship, the *Atheiste.* In an attempt to capture it, Captain Vere is seriously wounded. The French ship is defeated, and the British vessel manages to get to Gibraltar, where Captain Vere later dies. In the last moments before his death, the captain is heard to murmur, "Billy Budd, Billy Budd."

Although Claggart was exonerated and Billy Budd was executed as a traitor, the spirit of Billy Budd lives on. The common sailors do not forget their noble comrade. They keep trace of the spar upon which Billy had been hanged. "To them a chip of it [is] as a piece of the Cross."

LIST OF MAIN CHARACTERS

Billy Budd

Of obscure origin, a good-hearted and simple peacemaker, who because of his innocence and beauty is hated by Claggart.

Claggart

The dark, demon-haunted master-at-arms who because of jealously and hatred is the cause of Billy's execution.

Captain Vere

A man who through his sense of duty is forced to condemn Billy to death, although he sympathizes with Billy and recognizes his innate innocence.

The Dansker

With a long, pale scar across his face and a blue-peppered complexion, this old sailor is the one who warns Billy that Claggart is "down on him."

Squeak

A corporal aboard ship who gives Claggart false reports of petty offenses allegedly committed by Billy Budd.

SUMMARIES AND COMMENTARIES

NOTE: The reader may be puzzled to discover some textual differences in the various editions of *Billy Budd.* There is even disagreement in the form of the title and in the chapter divisions. This situation arises from the publishing history of the book. The work was never printed in Melville's lifetime but was left in the form of a rough manuscript containing many ambiguities and variant readings.

The book was first published in 1924. Since then, several scholars working from the original manuscript have prepared editions representing their best efforts to offer a version of *Billy Budd* that, in their opinions, is in accord with what were to be Melville's final intentions. The first of these editions was *Billy Budd, Foretopman,* ed. Raymond Weaver (New York: Horace Liveright, 1928). The chapterization in these Notes conforms with that of *Billy Budd (An Inside Narrative),* ed. Fredric Barron Freeman and revised by Elizabeth Treeman (Cambridge, Mass.: Harvard University Press, 1948, 1956). Since then has appeared

Billy Budd, Sailor (An Inside Narrative), ed. Harrison Hayford and Merton M. Sealts, Jr. (Chicago: University of Chicago Press, 1962).

CHAPTERS 1-2

Summary

Recalling the tradition of the Handsome Sailor, the author remembers seeing such a striking figure in Liverpool many years before, a native African of above-average height. Around his neck he wore a brightly colored scarf which fluttered against his dark chest.

Such a figure is the Handsome Sailor of this story, bright-eyed Billy Budd, aged twenty-one, a foretopman of the British fleet who had been impressed by Lieutenant Ratcliffe of the H.M.S. *Indomitable* from the English merchantman, the *Rights of Man*. Captain Graveling, of the latter ship, tells the impressment officer that before Billy came the "forecastle was a rat-pit of quarrels." Listening with amused interest, Lieutenant Ratcliffe gaily replies, "blessed are the peacemakers, especially the fighting peacemakers!" As the cutter pushes off, Billy jumps up from the bow and waves his hat to his shipmates looking at him from the taffrail, and bids the lads and the ship a genial good-by.

Billy is just as well received on H.M.S. *Indomitable* as he was on the *Rights of Man*. He scarcely notes the change of circumstances. Interrogated by an officer about his background and birthplace as he is being formally mustered into the service, Billy replies that he doesn't know. To the question of who his father was, Billy replies, "God knows, sir." The young man explains that he was found in a basket hung on "the knocker of a good man's door in Bristol." The author describes Billy as "little more than a sort of upright barbarian."

Perfect as this Handsome Sailor might appear, he does have just one noticeable weakness: when strongly provoked he is inclined to stutter, or he may even become speechless.

Commentary

Being in the age before steamships, the novel has a fairytale-like or fabulistic atmosphere. Associating the term Handsome Sailor first with the African and then with the hero of this story, Melville gives his novel a universality which is essential to its true meaning. Billy Budd enters human history at a time when order is threatened and the rights of man are at stake.

From the beginning Billy Budd is invested with superhuman attributes, many of them suggesting those of a Christ-like figure. Captain Graveling calls him his jewel and his peacemaker. To the surprise of all the crew Billy does not demur when he is impressed into the King's service by Lieutenant Ratcliffe. There is irony and pathos in Billy's impulsive but sincere gesture in jumping up in the cutter and bidding goody-by to "old *Rights of Man*." The lieutenant orders him to sit down, showing that Billy has indeed changed worlds, the world of peace and rights for the world of guns and military discipline.

There is also foreshadowed in this episode a preparation for the confrontation in which Billy strikes Claggart. Earlier aboard the *Rights of Man* Billy had been bullied by Red Whiskers. One day Billy struck a single stunning blow, possibly harder than he intended, and astonished the bully with his quickness. Since that day, Red Whiskers, as well as all the rest of the crew, has been his friend, for Billy is endowed with "the gaiety of high health, youth, and a free heart."

Billy's vocal defect—the fact that he stutters under extreme strain and pressure—is introduced here. This handicap has been interpreted in many ways, as original sin for example. It is this disability that causes Billy to take a life, and for that act he loses his own. Melville says that such an imperfection in the Handsome Sailor should be evidence "that he is not presented as a conventional hero," and that this story is not a romance.

CHAPTERS 3-5

Summary

In this year of 1797, there have been uprisings in the British navy, first at Spithead in April, then at the Nore in May. This latter episode was called the Great Mutiny. In fairness it must be said that many of the sailors who took part in the mutinies later serve heroically under Nelson at the Nile and at Trafalgar. Nelson dies at Trafalgar after writing his will, as though he has a premonition of his own death.

The *Indomitable* sails for the Mediterranean in these difficult times. Many of the abuses have been rectified, but impressment still continues, and every officer in the fleet watches for signs of discontent and trouble. Nelson, as the greatest naval hero of his time, has great personal influence over the men; but in battle, some officers still stand over the gunners with drawn swords.

Commentary

Every detail here and elsewhere in this finely wrought work of fiction is important and necessary to a full understanding of the story. In the early part of the novel, Melville explains current events and foreshadows those to come. The spirit of mutiny is in the air, and a conscientious and dedicated captain is forced to take this into account in dealing with the affairs aboard his ship.

Melville not only gives an accolade to Nelson, who obviously is one of his great heroes, but at the same time consciously or unconsciously prepares for an eventual comparison of this great naval commander with Vere, the captain of the *Indomitable.* Like Nelson, Captain Vere does not seek for personal glory and, like Nelson, he is "thoroughly versed in the science of his profession." In this historical setting the plot of the novel is placed and the destinies of the characters are decided.

CHAPTERS 6-7

Summary

Captain Vere, the Honorable Edward Fairfax Vere, a bachelor of about forty, has advanced in the service more by his own ability and bravery than through any family connections. Ever attentive to the welfare of his men, he has never tolerated any relaxation of discipline. A jovial kinsman bestowed on him the appellation "Starry Vere" upon his return from his West Indian cruise, where for his gallantry in action he had been advanced in rank.

Commentary

These chapters present Captain Vere to the reader. Introduced in the first, he is sketched out more fully in the following one. As far as appearance is concerned, ashore the captain could pass for a civilian. At sea on occasion he would exhibit a dreamy mood, absently gazing at the sea; yet he is capable of quick and courageous action.

In every way he is an exceptional man, with a taste for intellectual things. He loves books, and for this reason, some of his fellow officers find him "lacking in the companionable quality." Vere has a reserved and introspective nature, lacking in jocularity and the ability to engage in small talk. He is, however, self-controlled, law-abiding, and deeply concerned with his duties and responsibilities as an officer of the King's navy. His wide reading has been concerned with the affairs of men, and he opposes the current trend of political thought as being against the good of mankind. Vere's character is compared to the "King's yarn," the red strand running through all navy rope, symbolic of courage and devotion to duty, though his fellow officers making the comparison do not intend it to be complimentary.

The character of Captain Vere has been the subject of much critical attention. Interpretations vary, some critics considering him to be a fine professional officer caught in tragic circumstances, others believing that he is cold and heartless, seeking to enhance his reputation as a strict disciplinarian.

CHAPTERS 8-10

Summary

Among the petty officers on the ship is John Claggart, the master-at-arms, about whom many rumors fly concerning his mysterious background and his reasons for seeking sanctuary in the King's navy.

Billy Budd, having seen the gangway punishment, which happened the day following his impressment, given a young sailor who was away from his post when the ship was maneuvering, is determined that he will always perform his duties well, and that his actions will not be cause even for oral reprimand. Nevertheless, Billy finds himself getting into small difficulties on occasion. Perplexed, Billy goes to the Dansker, a veteran sailor who has taken a liking to Billy. After telling the old man his troubles, Billy asks for his opinion. The old man laconically replies, that Jemmy Legs (meaning the master-at-arms) is "down on him." Astonished, Billy protests that Claggart always speaks pleasantly to him. To this the old man cynically replies that that is because Claggart really dislikes Billy.

The day after this interview with the Dansker, Billy spills some soup on the freshly scrubbed deck just as Claggart passes by. Claggart steps over it and starts on his way without saying anything, when he notices that it was Billy who had caused the accident. At this Claggart's expression changes and, stopping just as he is about to reprimand Billy, he taps him lightly with his rattan, and remarks on Billy's little "trick." He moves on, leaving Billy bewildered by Claggart's apparent friendliness and by the Dansker's words which echo in his thoughts.

Commentary

These chapters introduce John Claggart, who is more fully developed, or rather analyzed, in subsequent chapters. One of the most interesting characters in the novel, Claggart has attracted wide attention from the critics, who have variously interpreted his character and his role in this drama of the soul.

Claggart's office aboard the man-of-war was not one to endear him to the crew. His advancement to this position from a lowly one was due to superior capacity, constitutional sobriety, and "ingratiating deference to superiors, together with a peculiar ferreting genius manifested on a singular occasion." This occasion is never explained by Melville.

Another important character is introduced in these passages. It is the old Dansker, the man of experience, who at first cannot believe that such innocence as Billy's is real and later is somewhat puzzled by the incongruity of such a one aboard the man-of-war. It is to this man that Billy Budd goes to find out the meaning of all that is going on about him. The old Dansker's intuitive knowledge can penetrate the smoke screen of action.

Experienced sailor that he is, the old Dansker can see through Claggart, and in his ascetic way has rather taken to Billy. He is one of the most important members of the crew, and, along with them, at various times functions as a chorus. Thus we learn, when Billy seeks him out, that he knows Claggart has strong, unreasoning prejudice against Billy—"Jemmy Legs is down on you."

CHAPTERS 11-14

Summary

To explain Claggart's animosity toward Billy Budd, one would have to look for something innate, an inborn wickedness, in Claggart. The point of the story turns on the hidden nature of the master-at-arms. With the exception of the captain, Claggart is the only person aboard who can recognize the moral phenomenon embodied in Billy Budd. This insight intensifies Claggart's envy of Billy.

Claggart apparently takes the spilling of the soup on the deck not as a simple accident, but as evidence of Billy's responsive dislike. Claggart's prejudice is fed by Squeak, one of his corporals, who has sensed his envy of Billy. Squeak's way of "ferreting" about the lower decks reminds the sailors "of a rat in a cellar." He makes up derogatory epithets which he tells Claggart are the sort of things Billy is saying about him.

Commentary

Melville begins the eleventh chapter with a series of questions. "What was the matter with Claggart," he asks. Whatever it is, how could it have any direct relation to Billy Budd, with whom he had never come into contact before the soup-spilling episode? Discarding the possibility of a prior meeting between the two, Melville muses on the mystery of "an antipathy spontaneous and profound." He rules out judging Claggart by the standards of normal behavior.

The thirteenth chapter utilizes one of Melville's most effective devices—contrast. He has used this device most effectively from the first page, when he vividly contrasts the black Handsome Sailor he once saw in Liverpool with the fair Handsome Sailor of this story. He contrasts the two ships, the names of which characterize them, and the captain of the *Rights* with the lieutenant (and by implication the captain) of the *Indomitable*. Later, youth and age are poignantly contrasted in the old Dansker and "Baby" Budd; the upper and lower decks are constantly mentioned, as are the ship and the land, sailors and civilians, the British fleet and the French fleet, and the warring elements in Claggart's personality—his envy of Billy, and his unreasoning hatred of him.

Envy and antipathy are called passions "irreconcilable in reason." Claggart envies Billy's good looks, good health, youth, and enjoyment of life, and most of all, perhaps, his honest, sincere innocence. This analysis by Melville of Claggart's mixed emotions and malice toward Billy, strange and real, has been called one of the finest things in this author's works.

CHAPTER 15

Summary

A few days after the soup episode the incidents of ill-omen that befall Billy approach their grim climax. One hot night he is sleeping on the upper deck when he is awakened by someone who whispers nervously to him to meet him at once on a secluded platform overlooking the sea, adding "There is something in the wind."

Billy complies, and is soon joined by the sailor who awakened him. In the "haze-obscured" starlight Billy cannot see the man's face clearly, but from his general physique recognizes him as one of the afterguardsmen.

Saying that he as well as Billy had been impressed into service, the sailor says that there is a gang of impressed men, and asks Billy to join them, offering him what appear to be gold coins. Angered, Billy stutters and threatens to throw the traitor over the rail. The repulsed conspirator quickly disappears.

Commentary

This is one of the most important chapters in the novel, for here occurs the crisis. Melville devotes the entire chapter to relating this final incident intended to complete Claggart's plan. Billy's doom is sealed. Claggart through his henchmen has obtained the evidence he needs, or so he thinks, to hang Billy.

Claggart's overt act in this chapter—for he is plainly the instigator—is one more in the age-old drama of the war between good and evil, waged in this case on the H.M.S. *Indomitable,* which becomes Melville's own symbol for the world. All of Claggart's other actions against Billy have been sly and devious; this one provides the means for his direct accusation of Billy Budd.

CHAPTERS 16-18

Summary

The mysterious nocturnal attempt by the afterguardsman to ensnare him in some implied mutinous venture deeply disturbs Billy Budd. A few nights afterward, as he is sitting on deck with the old Dansker, Billy tells his confidant the principal details without disclosing that the crewman is in the afterguard. The Dansker repeats his earlier charge that Jemmy Legs (Claggart) is down on Billy. When Billy then wonders what Claggart has to do with this traitorous afterguardsman, the Dansker instantly explodes that the traitor is just "a cat's-paw."

Billy is disinclined to attribute these peculiar incidents to Claggart. While he thinks the master-at-arms acts strangely at times, still he often greets Billy pleasantly enough. Billy is a simple, guileless sailor. When he becomes the object of suspicious glances from two messmates of Claggart, he is unaware of invidious implications. Billy fails to discern, through Claggart's calm surface behavior, his blazing internal malevolence—a sinister portent of disaster.

Commentary

Billy has learned little of evil, for he is inexperienced except in the ways of sailors. Obviously Melville thinks of Claggart as a citified man not at home on the sea; whereas Billy himself is the "old-fashioned sailor" and it is only such that he understands.

As the Dansker hints at disaster, Billy is insulated—if not protected—by his innocence, for it has not even occurred to him to report this traitorous act to his superiors. The monomania in Claggart's character, and the ambivalence of his attitude toward Billy, ominously forebode doom.

CHAPTER 19

Summary

Some days after Billy Budd's repulse of the attempted bribe, Captain Vere is approached on the quarterdeck by Claggart, and he asks the master-at-arms what he wants. In a lengthy, indefinite, circuitous accusation, Claggart tells the captain that one of the impressed sailors is a dangerous character who is involved in something clandestine among the crew, and who has acted strangely during a recent encounter with the enemy.

When Captain Vere impatiently interrupts Claggart's veiled allusions and demands that he name the dangerous crewman, Claggart says he is "William Budd." Captain Vere is astonished. Disbelieving Claggart's charges, he ponders the best way to dispose of the matter quietly. The long interview between Vere and Claggart on the quarterdeck has already been observed curiously by several officers, topmen, and other sailors.

Vere decides to bring Claggart and Budd unobtrusively to his cabin, where their confrontation may close the matter when Claggart's allegations are proved false. Vere sends his personal attendant to get Budd, and tells Claggart to stand by and follow Budd into his cabin.

Commentary

This chapter brings into fateful contact the two strongest characters in the novel. In the small, crowded, danger-fraught world embodied in the *Indomitable,* the captain and chief magistrate, Vere, is told by the master-at-arms, Claggart, that Billy Budd is a traitorous insurrectionist.

With the administrative ability developed through years of managing British warships and their unpredictable crews, Captain Vere quickly perceives that he is faced with a potentially flammable situation. His solution, the private confrontation in his cabin, is characteristic of a forthright disciplinarian. It sets the stage for the unexpected tragic denouement in the next chapter. Here we see the skilled writer's superb handling of his characters and situations.

CHAPTER 20

Summary

When Billy enters the captain's cabin and sees that Claggart is present, he is surprised but not alarmed. He wonders if the captain is going to make Billy coxswain, thinking that perhaps Vere is going to ask the master-at-arms about it.

Ordering the sentry to admit no one, Vere directs Claggart to tell Billy face to face the story he previously told the captain, alleging Billy's part in a conspiracy. Claggart walks up to Billy and with a hypnotic stare repeats his charge. Billy is speechless. When Vere orders him to speak in his own defense, Billy remains tongue-tied. Then Vere, sensing Billy's impediment, places his hand on Billy's shoulder and quietly tells him to take his time.

After an instant's further silence, Billy's right arm lashes out, striking Claggart on the forehead, and the master-at-arms falls to the deck, dead. With a whispered exclamation of shock and compassion, Vere tries with Billy's help to revive Claggart, but it is "like handling a dead snake."

Soon regaining his official composure, Vere orders Billy to wait in a rear stateroom. He sends for the ship's surgeon, who with one glance knows he is viewing a corpse, and then confirms it with the usual tests. The captain emotionally exclaims that Claggart is an Ananias, "struck dead by an angel of God" who must hang for his deed.

The captain and the surgeon put Claggart's body in the stateroom opposite Billy. Vere tells the surgeon he will quickly call a drum-head court, and to tell the ship's officers, but to request them to keep silent about what has happened.

Commentary

Ever mindful of form, and especially of symmetry of form, Melville follows the Shakespearean pattern of having the climax of his drama occur about the middle of the work. Manipulating his characters with a sure hand skilled at holding reader interest, Melville packs stark drama and tragedy into four fast-moving pages. Retribution destroys the demonic Claggart. Regrettably, the unintentional agent of vengeance is his intended victim, the simple sailor.

There is more action in this brief chapter than in the longest one in the story. Overcoming his immediate horror and personal sympathies, the professional captain resumes his official demeanor and skillfully arranges his management of affairs in the strict tradition of the King's navy. The action is all on stage. Melville arouses our interest as to what will happen next.

CHAPTERS 21-22

Summary

As he leaves the captain's cabin, the surgeon is disturbed. He disapproves of Captain Vere's move to call a drum-head court; yet "to argue his order to him would be insolence. To resist him would be mutiny." The lieutenants and the marine captain share the surgeon's surprise and concern.

The officers are of the opinion that the matter should be referred to the admiral. Privately, Captain Vere would also prefer to hold Billy as a prisoner until the ship rejoins the squadron. The captain is "no lover of authority for mere authority's sake," and he has no inclination to monopolize responsibility that he can properly leave to his superiors or share with others. He feels, however, compelled by a potentially explosive situation to act swiftly in obedience to "his vows of allegiance to martial duty."

The drum-head court is convened quickly. Billy is arraigned; Captain Vere is the only witness. The first lieutenant asks Billy whether he agrees with the facts the captain has stated. Billy replies that the captain tells the truth, but that it is not as the master-at-arms asserted, for he has been loyal to the King. He says he bore no malice toward Claggart and that he is sorry he is dead, for he did not mean to kill him.

The officer of marines asks Billy why the master-at-arms should lie so maliciously about him. Billy has no answer, and turns an appealing glance toward Captain Vere. After further questions from the court as to the mystery, Captain Vere says that it is a "mystery of iniquity" that has nothing to do with a military court.

In a lengthy summation Captain Vere tells the court they owe allegiance to the King and not to Nature. Leave Billy's soul to heaven, he urges, a court less arbitrary and more merciful than a martial one. He contends that Billy must hang under the law of the Mutiny Act. Billy is formally convicted and sentenced to be hanged at the yardarm in the early morning watch.

Commentary

The reader worries along with the surgeon as he carries out the captain's orders to alert the ship's officers. Has the captain lost his customary aplomb for dealing with tense situations?

Our study in contrasts here sets apart the correct demeanor —and underlying concern and compassion—of the officers who comprise the court-martial; the simplicity and defenselessness of the sailor; and the attitude and reasoned summing up of the captain as he presses the court in the name of the King for a death sentence in compliance with the Mutiny Act.

We might also see an ambivalence between the captain's own personal esteem for Billy and his unswerving devotion to duty. It may be said that Vere diminishes our respect for him as a human being by his condemnation of an accused man for whom there might have been a lesser penalty.

Yet it must be remembered that the *Indomitable* was far from the main body of the fleet, after encountering a French warship and barely escaping from the enemy craft. The military situation may—or may not—mitigate the readers' judgment of Captain Vere.

CHAPTERS 23-24

Summary

Captain Vere tells Billy privately of his conviction and sentence: to be hanged at the yardarm in the early morning watch. As the captain leaves the cabin the first to see him is the senior lieutenant, who sees in the captain's face an expression of suffering.

Less than two hours later the crew is summoned on deck. The captain tells them briefly and clearly what has happened—Claggart is dead; Billy Budd killed him, and has been tried and convicted; he is sentenced to hang, and the execution will take place early the next morning. As he finishes, a murmur arises from the crew, but it is ended instantly when the boatswain and his mates pipe down the watch.

Claggart's body is buried at sea according to the ritual and honors of his naval rank. Billy is guarded by a sentry, who is ordered to let only the chaplain see the condemned sailor.

Commentary

Melville's penchant for discursiveness through pages and pages of type is always under control. He can switch to dynamic brevity whenever it suits his purpose. In these brief chapters we get a fast wrap-up of the rituals of British naval procedure on a ship in wartime. All compassion spent, the officers and crew of the *Indomitable* go through with the rigid formalities of their grim duties.

Every detail of the regulations is rigidly observed. The condemned man is told his fate. His victim is lowered into the sea with the proper obsequies. Unobtrusive precautions are taken to prevent disorder. Meanwhile, one assumes, the *Indomitable* sails on on its assigned mission to rejoin the Mediterranean fleet.

CHAPTER 25

Summary

Having been transferred under guard from the captain's quarters to a space between two guns on the upper gundeck, Billy lies in irons, under surveillance of the sentry. Reclining "as in a trance," he is visited by the chaplain. Seeing that Billy is not aware of his presence, the chaplain goes away.

He returns again after midnight. Billy is awake now, and greets the chaplain. The chaplain tries without avail to impress upon Billy the theological abstractions of salvation and the after-life. The communication gap between the man of God and the simple sailor is a bridgeless chasm. Although he listens respect-fully, Billy simply does not know what the chaplain is talking about. The chaplain does not persist. After impulsively kissing the doomed man on the cheek, he reluctantly leaves Billy.

Commentary

This chapter is the key to an understanding of the main religious motif in the novel. It is significant that in the confronta-tion between the chaplain, or organized religion, and Billy Budd, the "upright barbarian" as Melville calls him, or Christ as some critics have called him, or "Adam before the fall" as he has been interpreted, or Isaac to Vere's Abraham – confrontation and not conference because Billy does not speak, but only listens politely – Melville reverts back to his *Typee* days to find a parallel. Billy's reaction to theological pronouncements reminds the author of the Tahitian savage of long ago when the first missionary arrived.

Irony so apparent everywhere in Melville's writing is not just implicit here; it is remarked upon by Melville himself, who describes the chaplain's strange behavior and marvels at the fact that, knowing the doomed man's innate innocence, he did noth-ing to try to save his life. In describing the prisoner early in this chapter, Melville again sounds the sarcastic note in an obvious attack upon war, upon profiteers, and upon hypocrisy.

The height of irony comes in the description of Billy, always the peacemaker and the epitome of innocence, lying between the two guns. He is now serene and resigned to his fate. Billy's brief agony, reminiscent of that of Christ's, does not outlast his conference with Vere after the trial and verdict. Then if Billy is symbolic of Christ here, the father-like captain is God. At any rate at this point Billy is at peace with Captain Vere and the world.

The efforts of the chaplain who comes to see him are useless. Billy is aware of his approaching death, but does not fear it. Here again is extreme irony. Why, in a highly civilized community which practices Christianity, a religion that so much stresses other-worldliness, should its adherents have an irrational fear of death which will transport them to bliss? This is what Melville seems to be saying.

CHAPTERS 26-28

Summary

All hands are summoned on deck to witness the execution. The prisoner is brought to the deck, accompanied by the chaplain. Billy stands facing the stern. At the last minute his words ring out clearly—"God bless Captain Vere!" These words have a phenomenal effect on the crew, which echoes—"God bless Captain Vere!"

The mystery of the absence of all bodily motion at the moment of Billy's death is surpassed by the complete silence at the instant of his execution, and for a brief time after that. This soundlessness is succeeded by a strange murmur emanating from the men massed on the ship's open deck, quickly halted by the piping down of the watch. The shrill shriek of sea hawks is heard later, as Billy's body, wrapped in his hammock, slides into the sea.

The drumbeat to quarters draws the men's attention from the scene of committal, and sends them to their various quarters or to their regular duties. The band on the quarterdeck plays a sacred air and the chaplain goes through the customary morning service.

Commentary

In these three chapters, the author establishes an atmosphere of somber tension. The procedure for execution, particularly of a favorite crewman, holds a grim potential for disturbance—emotional, and possibly physical. The normal morning routine, with its ingrained habits, is skillfully utilized at an earlier-than-usual hour to divert the crew's thoughts following the hanging and burial of Billy Budd. Melville deftly concludes the action of the main section of his yarn before going on to his rather routine final chapters.

CHAPTERS 29-31

Summary

Upon returning to the English fleet in the Mediterranean, the *Indomitable* encounters the French line-of-battle ship *Atheiste*. In the engagement that ensues Captain Vere is hit and seriously wounded by a musketball. He is succeeded in command by the senior lieutenant, under whose direction the enemy ship is finally captured. The lieutenant successfully takes both ships into Gibraltar, not far from the scene of the fight, and here Captain Vere, with the rest of the wounded, is put ashore. Dying, he is heard to murmur words inexplicable to his attendant—"Billy Budd, Billy Budd."

A few weeks after the execution of Billy Budd a notice appears in a naval chronicle stating that Claggart was stabbed by Budd. The account also states that the assassin was not an Englishman, but rather an alien taking an English name.

In the navy "any tangible object associated with some striking incident of the service is converted into a monument." The spar from which Billy was hanged becomes such a monument. The bluejackets have kept track of it. "To them a chip of it [is] as a piece of the Cross." They do not know the full story of the tragedy; nevertheless, they feel that the penalty was unavoidable, although they know intuitively that Billy could not be guilty of mutiny, any more than he could of willful murder.

Commentary

Billy Budd and *Typee* have much in common. This is especially evident in the respective endings. Once the plot has been completed in both novels, Melville feels compelled to attach a sequel to the work. As he says in Chapter 29 of *Billy Budd,* the first chapter of a three-chapter sequel, "something in way of sequel will not be amiss."

Apparently the author, who, like Hawthorne in his preface to *The Scarlet Letter,* insists that he is describing an actual incident, is not content to let his story end with the death of Billy Budd as it should naturally end, but adds a sequel in which he underlines the moral or meaning of his fable. He wants to get at the truth. Yet what he achieves even in the sequel is pure fiction.

In the body of the novel itself the three main characters each dominate through their presence or influence about a third of the novel respectively: Billy Budd the first part, Claggart the middle, and Captain Vere the last part (with the exception of Billy's conviction and execution). In the sequel the same situation prevails, for Captain Vere dominates the first chapter. It is all about his death, at which time he is heard to murmur "Billy Budd, Billy Budd" as if he might be blessing him or might be expressing a hope of joining him. At any rate these words are not uttered in remorse. Of course at his execution Billy Budd had said a benediction for Captain Vere.

The second chapter in the sequel is the most puzzling one and probably the one most crucial to Melville's true intent in the novel as a whole. As might be predicted, the character who dominates this chapter is John Claggart, who is immortalized in the account in the naval chronicle in a way he was never recognized in real life. From the point of view of the British fleet or of society he is seen as the hero of the *Indomitable* affair. Indeed he is in his glory. In the eyes of the world he and Billy Budd have changed places, just as they do earlier in the novel when Billy Budd, who is known as the peacemaker of the *Rights of Man*, is impressed into service aboard H.M.S. *Indomitable*, where John Claggart as master-of-arms is actually the peacemaker or keeper of the peace.

This entire account is ironic from beginning to end, with perhaps the most ironic or satiric part of all being Melville's first paragraph (Chapter 25), which assures the reader that though doubtless it was for the most part written in good faith, the way the story reached the writer tended to distort the facts. One has the feeling that here Melville is attacking many facets of civilized life, including the accuracy of the press, and especially, perhaps, is castigating the rumormongers that plagued him all his life.

Every item of information in the account of Claggart's bravery in uncovering the alleged seditious plot is false. The greatest irony of all is one of the closing statements in which the author of the article takes on Dr. Johnson's "peevish saying" that "patriotism is the last refuge of a scoundrel." One recalls the scene in Chapter 19 when Claggart brings false accusations against Billy. Patriotism *is* indeed the last refuge of a scoundrel!

Thus in the public view, Claggart is the one who has saved the British fleet from another serious mutiny at the terrific price of his life—his crucifixion at the hands of the depraved criminal. Here again the roles seem to be reversed, with Claggart cast into that of a Christ saving his fellow man. And *J. C.* are his initials. Melville may be satirizing formalized and false religion which depends so much on a front, on aspect and respectability—upon, in a word, every *outside* appearance.

The last of the three chapters concludes with a poem by another foretopman. The gist of this chapter, the shortest of the three (excluding the sailor's ballad), is that Billy has become a legend in the British fleet, the spar from which he was hanged has become a monument or shrine, and a chip of wood from this object is as precious as a piece of the Cross. The last word belongs to Billy, who has left an indelible impression on all.

CRITICAL ANALYSIS

The following analyses are meant to be suggestive, not definitive. The possibilities for analyzing and interpreting *Billy Budd* are limitless. Each new thought about this intricately wrought and richly complex novel provides the reader with a different and deeper insight into its meaning and implication. For the most part the comments that follow are not restricted to just one interpretation, but are a mélange of many. Naturally, since this is the case, it is inevitable that contradictory and conflicting views will be presented.

PLOT

Unlike *Typee*, which has almost no plot or serious action stemming from a basic conflict, *Billy Budd* has a very distinct plot, and for the most part a very simple one in view of the complexity of the moral concerns of the author. Billy Budd, the Handsome Sailor, having been impressed into the British navy to serve on board the *Indomitable*, encounters the mysterious hidden enmity of the master-at-arms, John Claggart, who accuses him of subversion. Facing his accuser and struck dumb by the accusation, Billy unwittingly kills Claggart. For this crime against the state Billy is convicted and sentenced to death.

Some attention should be given to Melville's label "an inside narrative" when one considers the plot of *Billy Budd*. First of all the action is restricted to the limited environment of the small world of the ship. Like the valley of the Typees, the *Indomitable* is cut off from the outside world. This is true to an even greater degree because she is at sea, and is separated from the main part of the fleet. Such spatial limitations magnify the forces of good and evil and limit the characters of the story in their interaction with men and nature.

The main action in *Billy Budd*, however, is primarily between Billy and Captain Vere, both of whom are ironic characters. Vere sees the evil in Claggart killed by the "blow of an angel." Ironically, Vere cannot consider the motives for Billy's action but must call for the trial, at which he urges the death penalty for the Handsome Sailor.

Structurally, the novel is built around the three main characters, with each one dominating about a third of the whole. However, Billy himself holds the novel together. He is present in every scene and in every thought, even after his death. The novel begins with a description of him aboard the *Rights of Man*. It reaches its dramatic climax in the confrontation between Billy and Claggart, and the height of its significance in the hanging of Billy, which is followed by the quiet description of his burial. With the death of Billy, however, Melville does not seem quite satisfied that he has achieved "the symmetry of form attainable in pure fiction." He therefore adds, in the last few pages, an interpretation of the theme and mood which he is trying to impart, for "truth uncompromisingly told will always have its ragged edges."

The overall pattern of plot movement in *Billy Budd* suggests classical tragedy. The protagonist is larger than life. Billy is compared to Achilles in his conversation with the Dansker, who functions here somewhat as a chorus. The blind fates determine that Billy is the one to be impressed from the *Rights of Man* and draw him to the time and place of the initial conflict. The action begins to build toward a climax at the moment Claggart intimates Billy's role in the conspiracy. The reader then is given a moment of false hope that Captain Vere will not believe Claggart's lying accusation. Following quickly is Billy's tragic mishap of fatally striking Claggart. Once again the reader has a moment of false hope at the court-martial when it seems as though Billy may not be convicted. Then these hopes are dashed as Billy is condemned and hanged.

At several places in the novel, the sailors also serve as a chorus, and the Dansker cryptically delivers the Delphic message to Billy, "Jemmy Legs is down on you." At the moment Claggart is struck down, Captain Vere whispers, "Fated boy." From the moment of Billy's hanging, there is falling action, until the novel comes to a close with the choric ode, "Billy in the Darbies."

To make the story suddenly leave the realm of Greek tragedy and enter the supposed realm of reality, Melville added three short chapters and the ballad, "Billy in the Darbies." These final chapters carry Billy's story forward. The first of these chapters records the death of Captain Vere some days after the capture of the *Atheiste*. His dying words are "Billy Budd, Billy Budd!" The second chapter records the ironic reversal of character and fact which was preserved in a weekly naval chronicle, under the heading "News from the Mediterranean." The last chapter traces the history of the yard from which Billy was hanged, reveals how chips of it came to be as cherished as pieces of the Cross, and records the composition of the ballad printed at Portsmouth.

The last three chapters in *Billy Budd* and the Appendix in *Typee* seem to have been added to make the stories appear closer to "reality" than they otherwise might. The final chapters in *Billy Budd* also serve the purpose of completing the myth. It was the memory of Billy Budd, not of Claggart or of Vere, that remained. The poem concluding the novel is written as if it were happening in Billy's mind.

Through the use of innumerable literary devices, Melville has unified his narrative and given meaning and order to it. Such devices include irony, symbolism, foreshadowing, suspense, biblical and mythological allusions, and figurative language. These will be discussed in detail later under style.

This is a horizontal novel in that it takes a rather straightforward path in time from the beginning to the end. It consists of thirty-one chapters balanced between action and comment, with maritime events of the years preceding 1797 and other historical, biblical, and mythological allusions interspersed throughout the pages of the novel. The author builds his action up to a climax in Chapter 23, in which Captain Vere informs Billy of the decision of the court. The concluding three chapters serve to show the effects of Billy's death on those who knew him, and the manner in which it will be remembered by those who did not. Although these three chapters may appear to be anticlimactic, they seem to indicate the author's conviction that life goes on and circumstances are absorbed in the march of history.

In the last chapter Melville reveals the immortality gained by the foretopman. The spar from which he was suspended was kept track of. To the sailors a chip of it was as "a piece of the Cross." They recalled the "fresh young image of the Handsome Sailor, that face never deformed by a sneer or subtler vile freak of the heart within. Their impression of him was doubtless deepened by the fact that he was gone, and in a measure mysteriously gone." Left behind are the lines of a ballad which "found rude utterance from another foretopman, one of his own watch."

Perhaps Melville is saying that the only real immortality is that which is attained in the literary world. If this is so, it would be the final and supreme irony of this ironic tale, since at the time of the writing of *Billy Budd*, Melville was as unknown as the day he set sail from Fairhaven on the *Acushnet* bound for the South Seas. Ironically, *Billy Budd* was to play a major role in the rescuing of this great symbolic writer from oblivion.

SETTING

The action of *Billy Budd* takes place aboard the H.M.S. *Indomitable*, a ship of the British navy, during the year 1797, beginning in July of that year. Short of men, the *Indomitable* has set sail to join the Mediterranean fleet. Billy is taken on this man-of-war because he has been impressed into His Majesty's service from the merchant ship the *Rights of Man*, named for one of Thomas Paine's political tracts. Billy's impressment from a ship so named sounds an ironic note at the very outset which is to be the dominant tone of the entire novel.

Although the setting of *Billy Budd* is a ship, the sea is, in effect, missing. The setting is rather the microcosm of a ship silhouetted against a background of war and mutiny at a time when insurgent democracy was the political theme and, in the words of Melville, "a period which, as every thinker now feels, involved a crisis for Christendom." The action occurs shortly after the "Great Mutiny" in the British navy at Spithead and the Nore. This fact complicates Billy's crime and perforce condemns him to be an example of wartime discipline, as Britain is at this time at war with France.

NARRATIVE TECHNIQUE

Classifying his tale as "an inside narrative" Melville tells the story by means of a shadowy narrator, referred to as "I" throughout. His identity is never revealed, his character never developed, nor is this necessary, for Melville may have intended himself to be thought of as the omniscient observer. If so, it is Melville, the complex artist working with imaginative material, and not Melville the man, who speaks alternately as witness and as commentator on events.

The author uses a shifting point of view in looking now into one character's mind, now into another's, in making general comments from time to time, in presenting scenes of dramatic action, and, when necessary, in shutting himself and the reader off from a scene entirely, such as in the intensely dramatic one between Billy and Captain Vere, in which the captain informs Billy that he must hang.

Following the preface, which informs the reader that the year is 1797 (twenty-two years before the birth of Melville), the opening chapter records, "In Liverpool, now half a century ago [Is the year here 1797 or is it 1888, the year he began Billy Budd?] I saw...a common sailor, so intensely black that he must needs have been a native African of the unadulterate blood of Ham....the center of a company of his shipmates." At the beginning of Chapter 4 in one of the numerous digressions for which the narrator apologizes and rationalizes by saying "in the matter of writing, resolve as one may to keep to the main road, some by paths have an enticement not readily to be withstood," the author addresses the reader.

This time, he explains, "I am going to err into such a by path." He continues, addressing the reader, "if the reader will keep me company I shall be glad. At the least we can promise ourselves that pleasure which is wickedly said to be in sinning, for a literary sin the divergence will be."

Having ended the story of "how it fared with the Handsome Sailor during the year of the Great Mutiny," which the narrator says "has been faithfully given," he appends to the narrative the sequel of three chapters with this explanation: "The symmetry of form attainable in pure fiction cannot so readily be achieved in a naration essentially having less to do with fable than with fact. Truth uncompromisingly told will always have its ragged edges; hence the conclusion of such a narration is apt to be less finished than an architectural finial."

By using a narrator who tells the story as though it were an actual occurrence, Melville succeeds in consciously forcing the reader to draw his own conclusions. In one such instance he says, "whether Captain Vere...was really the sudden victim of any degree of aberration, one must determine for himself by such light as this narrative may afford." Again at the death of Captain Vere, whose last words were, "Billy Budd, Billy Budd," other than to say that the words were not uttered in accents of remorse, the narrator offers no explanation why Billy Budd should haunt the captain, but leaves it to the reader to decide for himself.

CHARACTERS

Billy Budd

Melville introduces his three principal characters one by one at the time they enter the narrative. Having commented at some length on the prototype of the Handsome Sailor, whose comeliness, prowess, and masculine charm attract attention wherever he goes and win for him the admiration and homage of his less gifted associates, the narrator says "such a cynosure" in aspect and in nature is "welkin-eyed Billy Budd...aged twenty-one, a foretopman of the British fleet."

His characterization of the foretopman is one of Melville's major accomplishments. A youth of outstanding physical beauty and of sincere kindness toward all with whom he comes in contact, Billy exhibits the most ingenuous innocence, reflecting a complete unawareness of the existence of evil. In fact because of his innocent nature Billy is compared to "Adam before the fall." His only blemish is his tendency to stutter when he is under any type of emotional strain.

Wherever he goes he is acknowledged as peacemaker among men. For this reason, and for the role which he plays in the novel, Billy has been likened to Christ. His obscure origin accentuates his universality. It can also lead to speculation that Captain Vere could be his real father, a fact which would compound the irony of the tragic situation in which the captain feels compelled to urge the death sentence for his beloved son, with whom he is well pleased.

Claggart

If Billy is the apotheosis of all that is good, Claggart is the epitome of evil. The serpent in Billy's Eden, he is both Billy's tempter and his destroyer. Melville's comparisons of Claggart to Shawnee, treacherous enemy of the English colonists, to Titus Oates, diabolical plotter against Charles II, and to Ananias, shameless liar who was struck dead by God, clearly and concisely sum up his evil nature.

Melville uses more physical description in outlining this character than he used in that of Billy and the captain. Claggart is about thirty-five, we are told, somewhat thin and tall, "yet of no ill figure upon the whole." His small and shapely hands are not accustomed to hard work. His most notable feature is his face, "the features, all except the chin, cleanly cut as those on a Greek medallion." His cunning eyes cast "a tutoring glance." "His brow was of the sort phrenologically associated with more than average intellect; [with] silken jet curls partly clustering over it, making a foil to the pallor below, a pallor tinged with a faint shade of amber akin to the hue of time-tinted marbles of old." His appearance, the author concludes, seems "to hint of something defective or abnormal in the constitution and blood."

Claggart might well represent Satan, who tempted Adam with the sins of rebellion and disobedience. He is referred to in the novel as the serpent in the Garden of Eden. As he looks at Billy while bringing charges against him, Melville notes that "his first mesmeric glance was of serpent fascination." Later after Billy has struck the fatal blow, Captain Vere feels that moving Claggart's body is "like handling a dead snake." The fact that Melville leaves Claggart's background a mystery to the reader reinforces the idea that the master-at-arms represents an evil force that blasts the bloom of the young sailor.

Captain Vere

Of the three men, the most controversial is Vere. Like Claggart he is intelligent; but his intelligence, unlike Claggart's, has brought him wisdom rather than madness. Even his name, meaning "truth," conveys his character. He is Melville's complete man, his ideal man of action, mind, and heart. At all times he is a clear-thinking, thorough, and just commander. A man of forthrightness and frankness, he represents the synthesis of the heart and the intellect. Vere's most symbolic and controversial act is the trial and execution of Billy Budd, who seems like a son to him, because he puts the welfare of the state above natural law and personal feelings. He subordinates conscience to adherence to the code. Fearing the consequences if Billy's transgression is allowed to go unpunished, he persuades the drum-head court to suppress any personal feelings and to act for the larger good of society and the British navy. Loving Billy as a son he still realizes the necessity for Billy's death as a sacrifice to preserve the King's law. Caught between love and duty, he must choose duty.

THEME

Approximately four decades separate *Typee* and *Billy Budd*. As he did in the first work, Melville in his last novel again treats the ambiguities of life and the conflict of good and evil in the universe. The themes of *Billy Budd* thus are not greatly changed from those of *Typee*. The natural man is faced with the threat of destruction by an evil force he does not understand. The theme of the noble savage is as strong in *Billy Budd* as it is in *Typee*. That Billy was untutored in the ways of the world is apparent from his introduction up to his death, since Billy is described several times as a "barbarian."

As in *Typee*, the theme of *Billy Budd* seems to be the corruption of man by society. Melville seems to prefer the primitive state over civilized society. In this novel, too, we can see Melville still searching for the Garden of Eden inhabited by the noble savage.

In no other work by Melville is theme so important if we accept *Billy Budd* as Melville's last will and testament, as some critics do. Those looking for a final word from the long-suffering author see the novel's theme as an acceptance of and resignation to the imperfect life. Religion had always been full of contradictions and uncertainties for Melville. Finally in this terminal work he seems to accept things as they are and to adjust to the incongruities of life as a necessary tragic factor which he must endure. In this acceptance, though he never really finds the answer, Melville discovers a peace and understanding gained through suffering and reflection.

Randall Stewart in *American Literature and Christian Doctrine* sees in the novel a "brilliant and moving statement of the ultimate Christian lesson of resignation to God's overruling Providence." Stewart says Billy is "innocence," though not "perfection." He thinks that Captain Vere is a sympathetically drawn character, a practical man making necessary compromises in an imperfect world, between the "theoretically desirable and the practically attainable." According to Stewart the good and evil forces do not cancel themselves out in the struggle. A residue of good remains, the memory of Billy. Not only do the sailors revere Billy's memory, but even Captain Vere reverences it, most of all. His murmuring, "Billy Budd, Billy Budd," on his deathbed is "as if, Billy being a type of Christ, faith in Billy and his atoning death were the power of God unto salvation to everyone that believeth." Because as Christ blessed his enemies at his death, Billy blesses Captain Vere, Stewart feels that it is reasonable to think that Melville in his last days learned to subordinate his will to God's infinite judgment.

Thus, in line with Stewart's observation, the novel can be viewed as one in a long list that have used as their theme the crucifixion of the simple peacemaker who in a selfish world works to bring about the brotherhood of man. Inevitably he meets his death at the hands of his fellow man. Also, *Billy Budd* has been viewed as the tragedy of Everyman.

Using a somewhat different Christian interpretation, many critics have interpreted the theme symbolically as the fall of man. In this view Billy is seen as Adam, Claggart suggests Satan, and Captain Vere assumes the role of God. This theory finds some support in Melville's description of Claggart in serpentine terms as well as in overt comparisons of Billy to Adam.

It is not surprising that so complex a novel as this one, upon close analysis and determined probing, can reveal several probable themes. Undoubtedly the most obvious one is that Melville seeks and finds a final answer to the problems of good and evil. Evil is the ultimate victor and takes its place alongside good, but natural goodness remains unconquered in the heart of man. The problem of the destruction of innocence and good is tied up with the problem of evil in the world: unmitigated evil, unexplained, unmotivated, impossible of understanding. Billy himself is the symbol of innocence. Unaware of the evils of life, he is hopelessly unfitted for existence in the world of men.

The comparison of the two irreconcilable parts of Claggart's nature to Chang and Eng, the famous Siamese twins of the nineteenth century who were joined together in life and in death, suggests still another theme to this mysterious and complex tale. The two represent the two sides of the nature of man. Good and evil exist side by side. In one case the heart rules; in the other case the head rules. To be dominated by either one is dangerous. Like Aristotle's golden mean, the mean of these two extremes is to be preferred. Again, this mean may be represented by Captain Vere, in whom the two meet in perfect proportion. He is opposed to innovation and change, not because such tendencies are inimical to the privileged classes to which he belongs, but because "they seemed to him incapable of embodiment in lasting institutions, but at war with the peace of the world and the true welfare of mankind." He is truly the balanced man.

Some critics view the story as a commentary on the impersonality and essential brutality of the modern state, exacting the death penalty of the innocent. Billy is doomed through his innate innocence. Melville states: "He had none of that intuitive knowledge of the bad." Another theme is the problem of man's place in a hostile universe.

The setting of the novel aboard the *Indomitable* suggests the ship of life, or civilized society, in which innocence is doomed. The sea is the stream upon which mortal life is borne.

Richard Chase reduces the theme to a blunt assertion: "The real theme of *Billy Budd,*" he insists, "is castration and cannibalism, the ritual murder and eating of the host."

Others interpreting the theme primarily in terms of satire and irony stress the paradox at the center of the story that the *Rights of Man* cannot operate in the sea of life without the protection of the *Indomitable,* the usurper of those rights. In turn the *Indomitable* can protect the *Rights* only at the expense of impressing men from the ship it protects. Along the same lines Melville seems to be saying that the common man cannot understand the need for justice to rule in time of revolt.

The hanging of Billy Budd is Melville's final commentary on one theme: the impracticability of absolute standards in a world ruled by expediency. Billy's instinctive affinity for right and justice makes him the personification of natural law. His death means that his standard is unworkable when applied to a complex social relationship.

The frequent allusion to history, and his placing the action in "a crisis of Christendom not exceeded in its undetermined momentousness at the time by any other era whereof there is record," would indicate that Melville is concerned with the historical development of mankind and sees Christianity as the center of an order which seems to be gradually slipping away. This, as well as the other ideas mentioned above, seems to have been uppermost in his mind as in his declining years he penned this final work, which he dedicated to Jack Chase "wherever that great heart may now be here on earth, or harboured in Paradise." That Melville ever attempted to deal with this problem attests to his greatness.

STYLE

In almost all respects *Billy Budd* is a typical Melville production. It is a sea story, the author's favorite genre; it treats rebellion, directs attention to needed reforms (impressment), contains rich historical background, abounds in Christian and mythological allusions, concentrates its main action upon actual incidents, and concerns ordinary sailors. Everywhere the style is unmistakably that of Melville. The story is rife with mythic figures, stories, and analogues. So extensive is the use of allusion that *Billy Budd* is inevitably interpreted allegorically.

Although the language is prose, the rhythm often suggests poetry. Figurative speech abounding in metaphors and similes enriches the meaning as well as the diction of the novel. When Billy is accused by Claggart, he looked "struck as by white leprosy." At Billy's death the sky was "shot through with a soft glory as the fleece of the Lamb of God."

The sentences are long, the chapters short, often producing an impression of completeness. Foreshadowing, suspense, symbolism, irony, poetic diction, suggestive words, digressions, images, and distortions are some of the other techniques and devices which Melville employs to advantage in this short novel. The story develops simply, always unhurriedly, yet the action never lags. Each character is described with patience and care. By making the story so short, Melville has shown himself as a writer at his very best in his deepest, most poetic, and therefore most conscious style.

Most of the writing is exposition. In the novel we are told about the events in their sequential order but from a retrospective point of view rather than by means of the diary type narrative which Melville used in *Typee*. Although the novel is short on dramatic scenes, Melville's power in narrating the single incidents is unsurpassed.

Eager to have the reader believe that both *Typee* and *Billy Budd* are faithful accounts of actual happenings, Melville, after carrying the reader through the story of *Billy Budd* on high notes of some of the most imaginative prose in all of literature, ends the narrative in a matter-of-fact, drab, uninspired journalistic style.

The newspaper account of the so-called mutiny aboard the *Indomitable* is realistic. In its distortion of the fact, we see the reality of our own world. By telling us that the poem, "Billy in the Darbies," was not only published, but that it was published at Portsmouth, and that it was written by a friend of Billy's, a fellow foretopman, Melville jars us awake from our mythic nightmare and assures us that what we are witnessing are the cold facts of reality.

One critic has called the style of *Billy Budd* "the stiff and angular vocabulary of specification" (Warner Berthoff). Melville's style had matured from the flowery and fluid passages in *Typee* to a more dignified and sedate prose in *Billy Budd.* The sentences, long and somber, are packed—almost too full—with information.

The digressions play an important role in the structure and style of the novel. Spaced as they are, they have the same effect as the prophetic sound of the minor chord in the overture of an opera. Used at strategic moments, they often give pertinent background to illuminate a particular event. Melville's suggestive images give depth and scope to the plot and to the characters. His comparing Billy to Adam at one time and to Casper Houser at another time foreshadows the Handsome Sailor's fate. Billy's salutation and valediction to his old ship foreshadow his treatment aboard the *Indomitable:* "And good-bye to you too, old *Rights of Man.*" Claggart's character is illumined by an allusion to British history and to the Bible, "The Pharisee is the Guy Fawkes prowling in the hid chambers underlying some natures like Claggart's." In his digression on Admiral Nelson, Melville gives an insight into the character of Captain Vere, his outstanding ability and inflexible nature. By his artistic use of imagery and symbolism Melville gives his characters universality as well as vividness and verisimilitude.

Melville's narrative method in *Billy Budd* involves the technical principle of sustained irony. Irony involves contrast, a discrepancy between the anticipated and the actual. It involves paradox, a statement actually self-contradictory or false. In addition to using irony of statement, Melville also uses irony of situation involving a discrepancy between what we expect the outcome of an action to be—what would seem to be the fitting outcome—and the actual outcome. One critic thinks that Melville cunningly creates the artistic illusion that the narrator in *Billy Budd* sympathizes throughout with the authoritarian viewpoint of Captain Vere when in point of fact he does not (Lawrence Thompson).

Irony is seen throughout the pages of the novel. At the beginning of the novel Billy is taken forcibly from a ship called the *Rights of Man* and is impressed into the British navy. It is one of the paradoxical ironies of the story that the *Rights of Man* cannot operate on the sea unless it is protected by the *Indomitable,* the abridger of those rights. In turn the *Indomitable* can perform its protective function only by taking men by force from the ship which it protects. Billy's cry of "God bless Captain Vere" is a crowning irony. The sailors blessed Billy, not Vere, with Billy's words, "God bless Captain Vere." There is irony in Captain Vere's deathbed utterance, "Billy Budd, Billy Budd." Billy was hanged as a criminal, but was immortalized as a saint. There is irony in the false account in the naval chronicle which sees Billy as the saboteur and Claggart as the savior of the ship. There is irony in the fact that Claggart, desiring Billy's defeat by his false accusation, succeeds in bringing about his own death.

It is ironic, too, that in attempting to clear Billy by confronting him with his tormentor, Captain Vere is instrumental in causing Billy's death. Ironic, also, is the fact that Billy as the Handsome Sailor is perfection personified except for one small blemish, and it is this tragic flaw that brings about his downfall. Until his death Billy is unable to believe that Claggart could wish him harm, for he keeps saying that Claggart has always been kind to him and has always spoken favorably of him. Most ironic of all is the fact that John Claggart, who is generally regarded as the apogee of evil, bears the same initials as Jesus Christ, usually a dead give-away in modern fiction of the Christ-figure (Joe Christmas, Jim Casey, Jim Conklin).

The fact remains, however, that of all stylistic devices which Melville uses so effectively in this novel, the most important is symbolism. The symbols are predominantly biblical. Confused by its complexities and contradictions, Melville pondered all his life on the matter of religion. He annotated with constant care his copy of the New Testament. In all of his writing except a few short pieces echoes of the Bible can be heard. Statistics have been compiled to show that in *Billy Budd* alone there are some hundred allusions and twenty-two direct references to the Bible.

Frequently in his prose he even uses biblical phrasing. Foremost among the symbols are those of Christ and the Crucifixion, with Billy serving as Melville's Christ. Billy is not perfect, however, since he has a flaw—a stammer—which may be interpreted as symbolic of original sin. In spite of the defect, however, Billy's character conveys the idea that his soul belongs to the heavenly and not to the earthly world, and this is readily apparent to the chaplain of the *Indomitable*.

Billy has also been seen as Adam before the fall. He is compared with the Christian hero who, through resignation to his fate, finds solace in a heavenly reward. His innate goodness make him Christ-like. He is a peacemaker, and is so labeled by the good captain of the *Rights of Man*. Like Jesus, the young sailor hesitates to defend himself before the judges, and like Him alone with his Father in the Garden of Gethsemane, Billy has his moment with Captain Vere in the cabin before his death.

At the trial Billy's purity of conscience cannot be considered; he is convicted solely for his unpremediated act. His fate is similar to the one Jesus suffered. Under strict codes, the Mosaic Law and the Mutiny Act, the two were condemned to death. The courts that try them realize that the charge is only superficial. Billy dies with a prayer upon his lips, as did Jesus. Billy's prayer is, "God bless Captain Vere!"

At Billy's death all nature is affected, and the appearance of the sea and sky is phenomenal. In Melville's beautiful description of the sky is the suggestion of both the Ascension and the doctrine of the Atonement: "At the same moment it chanced that the vapory fleece hanging low in the East, was shot through with a soft glory as the fleece of the Lamb of God seen in mystical vision; and simultaneously therewith, watched by the wedged mass of upturned faces, Billy ascended; and, ascending, took the full rose of the dawn."

Another unnatural, awe-inspiring act occurs when Billy, wrapped in his sailor's hammock, is buried at sea. "A second strange human murmur was heard—blended now with another inarticulate sound proceeding from certain larger seafowl... [that] flew screaming to the spot.... As the ship under light airs passed on, leaving the burial spot astern, they still kept circling it low down with the moving shadow of their outstretched wings and the cracked requiem of their cries."

To strengthen the Crucifixion image even further, at the end of the novel, Melville writes that of the spar from which Billy was hanged even a chip of it was to the sailors "as a piece of the Cross." Billy's influence and significance are even more keenly felt after his death.

Captain Vere, whose name means truth, corresponds to the God-the-Father concept of the Crucifixion story. He has been seen by some scholars to represent Divine Justice and by others to personify Cosmic Tyranny. God himself, however, was willing for Jesus to die. Vere, in administering the law, is likewise bound by it. Too, he resembles Pontius Pilate, in that he condemns to death a man whom he feels to be innocent; unlike Pontius Pilate he does not wash his hands of the matter. According to the apocryphal story, the death of Jesus haunted Pilate to his own death. He lived out his last years as praetor to Hispania Tarraconensis. Nearby is Gibraltar, where Vere dies as he utters the name of Billy Budd. His ship, the *Indomitable,* has just conquered the French man-of-war *Atheiste.* Vere has also been seen as Abraham to Billy's Isaac. In the scene in which Billy confronts Claggart and is accused, he is comforted by the captain, who urges him to take his time in replying. This fatherliness so deeply touches Billy's heart that his face becomes, as Melville states, "a crucifixion to behold."

Again when Vere visits Billy before the execution, the reader can only surmise what takes place, but Melville implies there is sympathy, love, and respect between the two men. They meet as equals, evidently conceal nothing, and in a peculiar sense become one being. "The austere devotee of military duty, letting himself melt back into what remains primeval in our formalized humanity, may in the end have caught Billy to his heart." Billy's sole concern has been to rectify himself in the eyes of the captain. When he accomplishes this goal, he is wholly without irrational qualms concerning death. The chaplain, visiting him later, finds him possessed of such an astonishing and ineffable peace that he slips away, feeling no need for giving spiritual consolation.

In a Christian frame of reference the spiritual antithesis of Billy Budd is Claggart, symbolically Judas Iscariot, or the serpent in the Garden of Eden, another Ananias, or Satan himself. When Claggart is felled by Billy's reflex blow, Captain Vere exclaims, "It is the divine judgment on Ananias!" A moment later he exclaims, "Struck dead by an angel of God! Yet the angel must hang!"

Even in death, Claggart is serpentine. When Captain Vere and Billy attempt to lift it, the "spare form flexibly acquiesced, but inertly. It was like handling a dead snake." This strangely cold and calculating accuser has destroyed himself just as Judas had done.

Melville uses color symbolically in this novel. He pits the blond Billy against the black-haired Claggart. He speaks of the rose-red hue of Billy's complexion and of the sallowness of Claggart's. Billy lives in the light of the upper deck, while Claggart lurks in a dark and forebidding world below. Good and evil are thus reflected through an adroit manipulation of color.

REVIEW QUESTIONS AND ESSAY TOPICS

1. Is *Billy Budd* a unified novel? If so, where does the unity lie—in the characters, the plot, the theme, the style?

2. Why in the beginning does the narrator introduce the black Handsome Sailor whom he had seen on the docks of Liverpool half a century before?

3. Describe the plot structure of the novel.

4. Explain the different uses of irony in the novel.

5. What is the climax of the novel? Where does it occur?

6. How does the setting, particularly the time of the story, influence the outcome of the novel?

7. Are the names of the ships significant? What do they imply?

8. What qualities does Billy possess that make most people take an instant liking to him?

9. Explain why Billy quietly accepts his impressment.

10. What part does Billy's vocal impediment play in the story?

11. What is Billy's attitude toward Captain Vere, who tells him of his death sentence?

12. If the court believes in Billy's innate innocence, why does it sentence him to be hanged?

13. Why does the chaplain go away and leave Billy alone the night before his death?

14. What is the reaction of the sailors on the *Indomitable* to Billy's death?

15. What is meant by the ballad at the end of the novel?

16. What is Captain Vere's nickname and how did he acquire it? Do the names of the other characters have any special significance?

17. Do you think Captain Vere's actions throughout the story are in keeping with his character? Explain.

18. What is Captain Vere's reaction when Claggart approaches him on the subject of Billy's involvement in a mutiny?

19. What does the captain see as Billy's real crime?

20. What is significant about Captain Vere's death?

21. What is Claggart's position on board ship and how does he utilize this position?

22. What motivates Claggart in his attempt to destroy Billy?

23. What is the Dansker's attitude toward life?

24. What use does Melville make of biblical and mythological allusions in the novel?

25. What commentary on civilization does Melville make in *Billy Budd*?

SELECTED BIBLIOGRAPHY

AUDEN, W. H. "Claggart 1," in *Melville's Billy Budd and the Critics*. Ed. WILLIAM T. STAFFORD. Belmont, Calif.: Wadsworth, 1961. A discussion of "pride" and its denial of the six other deadly sins in Claggart, the Devil.

BERNSTEIN, JOHN. "*Billy Budd:* The Testament of Rebellion," in *Pacifism and Rebellion in the Writings of Herman Melville*. London: Mouton, 1964. Takes the view of *Billy Budd* as being a "Final Irony." A discussion of pacifism and rebellion themes in Melville's works.

BRASWELL, WILLIAM. "Melville's *Billy Budd* as 'An Inside Narrative.'" *American Literature*, XXIX (May, 1957), 133-46. An essay commenting on *Billy Budd* as a spiritual autobiography centered upon tragic conflict in Melville's own life.

CASPER, LEONARD. "The Case Against Captain Vere," in *Melville's Billy Budd and the Critics*. Ed. WILLIAM T. STAFFORD. Belmont, Calif.: Wadsworth, 1961. Critical opinions concerning Captain Vere's character and actions.

CHASE, RICHARD. "The Rite of Sacrament," in *Melville's Billy Budd and the Critics*. Ed. WILLIAM T. STAFFORD. Belmont, Calif.: Wadsworth, 1961. A critical study of Melville: myth, symbolism, and the idea of Billy as Host.

FOLEY, MARY. "The Digressions in *Billy Budd*," in *Melville's Billy Budd and the Critics*. Ed. WILLIAM T. STAFFORD. Belmont, Calif.: Wadsworth, 1961. An essay explaining the digressions in the novel.

HILLWAY, TYRUS. *Herman Melville*. New York: Twayne, 1963. (United States Author Series, No. 37). A biographical and critical discussion of Melville and his works.

MURRAY, JOHN MIDDLETON. "Five Early Views," in *Melville's Billy Budd and the Critics*. Ed. WILLIAM T. STAFFORD. Belmont, Calif.: Wadsworth, 1961. One of the early critiques (1924) on *Billy Budd* as the last will and spiritual testament of a man of genius.

STERN, MILTON. *The Fine Hammered Steel of Herman Melville*. Urbana, Ill.: University of Illinois Press, 1957. A study of Melville's basic attitudes toward life and his main philosophical theme—cosmic and anti-idealistic "naturalism." Also a helpful checklist of Melville studies.

WEAVER, RAYMOND. "Five Early Views," in *Melville's Billy Budd and the Critics*. Ed. WILLIAM T. STAFFORD. Belmont, Calif.: Wadsworth, 1961. An earlier essay (1921) on Melville's study of the evil in Claggart.

"Typee" Notes

BRIEF SYNOPSIS

Typee owes its source to Melville's experiences as a sailor aboard the *Acushnet*, a whaling vessel, and his adventures in the South Sea Islands. It is told in the first person by Tom, or Tommo as the natives called him, since they could not pronounce the shorter form. In Nukuheva Bay he decides to jump ship because of an intolerable situation aboard the *Dolly*—poor food, hard work, and a tyrannical captain. Toby, a fellow sailor, agrees to leave with him and to share the escape and subsequent adventure.

Intending to seek asylum with the friendly Happars, the two sailors miss their way and find themselves instead in the Typee valley, where they are well received and well treated. The abundant food which they are given is eaten under some apprehension that they are being fattened for a feast. All of their attempts to depart are frowned upon and actually thwarted. Other than this restriction they have no cause to complain of their treatment. Suffering from a sore leg, Tommo is nursed by the lovely Fayaway and attended day and night by the faithful Kory-Kory.

Toby, in seeking medical aid for his ailing companion, becomes separated from him and disappears. For four months Tommo lives an indolent, luxurious life in this island paradise with nothing to do, with plenty to eat, waited on by his body servant, Kory-Kory, petted by a score of the beautiful young Eves of the island, and especially adored by the incomparable Fayaway. Tommo makes acute observations of the social, religious, and moral customs of the natives. When the tribe insists he be tattooed, he is aroused to discontent and to consider departure or escape; also, he fears that the cannibals may turn from eating their enemies, the Happars, to eating white men. Tommo, moral American, choosing to return to civilization, regretfully leaves his island love.

Rescued by Karakoee, a native of Oahu whom he had known aboard the *Dolly* at Nukuheva, Tommo escapes aboard an Australian whaler, and eventually makes his way home.

In a sequel the reader learns that Toby, taken off the island in a passing ship, had also returned safely.

CRITICAL ANALYSIS

This analysis makes no pretense to completeness or authoritativeness. It aspires at most to an exploration and re-evaluation of the most neglected item in Melville's canon. Admittedly, *Typee* is a simple tale concerning which not much profound can be said. However, it is a work of literature that lends itself to stimulating discussion and finds importance in the fact that it represents Melville's first sally into the world of print. Whatever place it holds in American literature, it remains Melville's initial success and provides us with our first insight into the mind of this literary genius.

PLOT

Many critics believe that Melville's first book makes no claim whatever to being a novel. It is, according to their view, travel literature with no plot, no central action, and no basic conflict. The structural development of *Typee* is not complex. At no place do we see the hand of the artist firmly in control of his material. Events move him; he does not shape or move them. But a novel it is.

Typee illustrates the horizontal form of novel, or to a degree the travelogue, which it resembles, with events following in chronological order and suspense a key factor in holding the reader's interest. We become aware of the story of the novel through the revelation of episodes told in sequence, an actual day-by-day account of Tommo's experience on the island. Much more is involved, however, than lush descriptions and hourly reports.

The plot, though far from being intricate, does exist. Tommo, through whose eyes we see the action and view the scenery, a latter-day Adam seeking a nineteenth-century Paradise, blunders into an unspoiled Eden. He and his companion in adventure, Toby, having jumped ship to escape the frustrations of civilized society symbolized by the brutal captain and hardened crew of the *Dolly,* struggle to reach the boundary of the peaceful Happars only to find themselves in the domain of the dreaded Typees. Suspense and romance enter the narrative as the two wanderers, captives really, fear that they will be the next victims of these cannibals, and when Tommo falls in love with the beautiful and enchanting Fayaway, in whose company he spends many pleasant hours.

Toby's mysterious disappearance in search of medicine for Tommo's sore, lame leg causes Tommo to fear for his safety more than ever. Although his hosts treat him with the greatest respect and kindness, he is determined to quit the island. With the help of Marnoo, a taboo islander, he barely escapes with his life. The plot thus reveals all the essentials for exciting action, exploration, discovery, and flight. Much of the action occurs in Tommo's mind, the turmoil there and the tension involved in making the difficult choice between Typee society or the Western world.

The novel presents three main actions, two of which involve escape. The first part of the novel describes life aboard the *Dolly* and deals with Tom and Toby's escape from the ship. The major part, however, concerns Tommo's life in the Typee valley. This part can conveniently be described in five sections. The first one describes the arrival of the two fugitives in the Typee valley. The second concerns Toby's departure. The third depicts a typical day in the Typee valley. The fourth records Marnoo's visit. In the fifth section Tommo becomes convinced that the natives are cannibals. The third and last part of the novel recounts Tommo's escape from the valley. To this well-formed structure Melville appends a sequel to inform the reader of Toby's rescue and safe arrival in this country.

SETTING

In a Melville novel the sea is usually not far away, and the world is usually too much with us. Such is the case in *Typee*. The setting for most of the book is on Nukuheva, one of the islands of the Washington Group of the Marquesas Islands in the South Pacific. More specifically the setting in Chapter 1 is aboard the American whaler the *Dolly*. In Chapter 2 the ship is in the Bay of Nukuheva. In Chapter 3 the setting is the mountains of Nukuheva. In Chapter 9 the two deserters reach the beautiful and exotic valley of the Typees. This remains the setting until Tommo's escape at the end of the novel from his captives back to the sea to an Australian ship, the *Julia I*.

The chronological ordering of events covers a four-month period in the lives of the two malcontents in the summer of 1842. In the beginning the narrator gives the background and traces the ship's recent voyage around Cape Horn. Having been at sea for six weary months, the narrator says he "can never forget the eighteen or twenty days during which the light trade-winds were silently sweeping us toward the islands." The sequel, however, goes back in time to explain what happened to Toby.

POINT OF VIEW

The episodes are related by Melville through the narrator, his autobiographical creation Tommo. The point of view is both that of the young romantic wanderer experiencing each new adventure and that of the older and more mature writer recalling events as they happened four years earlier.

Although the story for the most part is told in the past tense, the direct narrative portions are told in the present. Chapter 4 begins with the statement, "our ship had not been many days in the harbor of Nukuheva before I came to the determination of leaving her." He abandons his narrative to address the reader: "I may here state; and on my faith as an honest man, that though more than three years have elapsed since I left this same identical vessel, she still continues in the Pacific...." Then he remembers, "But to return to my narrative," and again later in the novel, "For my own part, I am free to confess my almost entire inability to gratify any curiosity that may be felt with regard to the theology of the Valley. I doubt whether the inhabitants themselves could do so."

The actions of the characters are described through the use of the present participle. At the beginning of Chapter 30, Melville recounts, "In one of my strolls with Kory-Kory, in passing along the border of a thick growth of bushes, my attention was arrested by a singular noise. On entering the thicket I witnessed for the first time the operation of tattooing as performed by these islanders." Such skillful manipulation of subtle syntactical tense and construction gives a sense of immediacy to the scene.

CHARACTERS

In *Typee* Melville's characters are at the most just hastily drawn sketches. There is little or no development of characters. Melville uses his autobiographical hero, **Tom**, or **Tommo** as he is called by the Typees, to set forth his own views. For this reason he has been called less of a man than a "capacity for perception." Displaying little interest in his main character, Melville does succeed in establishing Tommo's chief trait. He is a wanderer, a searcher, a seeker after unattainable happiness and security, one who desires to escape from reality, from the pain and responsibility of civilized society. He is, in short, a romantic.

Toby, Tommo's companion and fellow fugitive, is a little better drawn. He, too, is a traveler, a sea rover whose wanderings over the world give the impression that he is inescapably fated for this role. He never reveals his origin or talks about his home. Courageous, mysterious, and moody, he is at one moment extremely melancholy and at the next given to a display of fiery temper.

Among the minor characters portrayed also in a static way are Fayaway, Kory-Kory, Mehevi, Marheyo, and Marnoo. These savages are gentle and generous to Tommo compared with the "ravening wolves" of his "white brothers." They are happy in their primitive state, just as Billy Budd is happy in his innocence. But Melville makes plain his disgust with their animal-like existence, devoid of mind and spirit and enjoyment of pleasures without ascertaining their origin or meaning.

By far the most attractive of the "savages," **Fayaway**, the young native girl, spends many happy hours with and offers many sensual pleasures to Tommo during his stay among her people. Extremely beautiful, graceful, gentle, she is the epitome of femininity. In comparing her natural beauty with that of European women, Melville finds her type much more appealing. She possesses an atmosphere of perpetual summer.

Kory-Kory, whose grotesque appearance, caused by the intricate tattooing on his face and his native-style haircut, is a constant companion to the semi-captive Tommo. He is both his guard and his lackey, whose generosity, thoughtfulness, and constant attention to every wish and whim of his guest knows no limits. He is the son of Marheyo, in whose household Tommo is detained and entertained. **Marheyo** is just as solicitous of Tommo's needs and desires as his son is. He is an animated, comic, fussy old busybody who dreams up ways of making Tommo happy.

Perhaps the most interesting character in the novel, however, and the most significant one in view of Melville's future development is **Marnoo**, a twenty-five-year-old "Polynesian Apollo," a taboo kanake who is accorded the special privilege of traveling from valley to valley without fear of being harmed. He has been called the "true Prometheus, the heroic voyager whom Melville later called the Handsome Sailor" and is seen as the prototype of Billy Budd.

Melville employs this primitive setting and these typical natives to compare the good and bad that exist in all men. Further Melville shows certain human foibles that are present in both civilized and primitive societies the author describes. Tinor, the mother of the household where Tommo resides, was always busy even when there was no need to be busy. "She was a genuine busybody, bustling about the house like a country landlady at an unexpected arrival; forever giving the young girls tasks to perform, which the little hussies as often neglected; poking into every corner, and rummaging over bundles of old tappa, or making a prodigious clatter among the calabashes."

Universal traits are also revealed when Melville describes the natives busily preparing to meet one of the boats. While many were picking fruit to sell or weaving baskets to market the fruit in, Tommo notices that "as in all cases of hurry and confusion in every part of the world, there were a number of individuals who kept hurrying to and fro, with amazing vigor and perseverance, doing nothing themselves, and hindering others."

The vivid descriptions of the islands and the lush valley of the Typees are equally matched by those of the exotic and picturesque natives themselves. Thus the variety of settings in the novel and the large number of characters introduced into the narrative restrict their development. Melville never develops any of his characters, even the beautiful, charming, delightful, and irresistible Fayaway, in spite of the fact that they spend a great deal of time together. Neither are Toby or Kory-Kory or Mehevi developed to any degree beyond what the story demands. The purpose of introducing Toby, in addition to adding suspense and creating mystery, is to provide a contrast with the romantic Tommo, as Toby is the rational man.

THEME

Even in his first novel Melville provides no clear-cut explanation or specific statement of his intent and theme. He allows his reader the privilege of deciding for himself the meanings and implications embedded in the narrative. Yet here at the beginning of his career Melville makes it plain that one of his major themes, if not the primary one, is that of primitive man versus civilized society. This is the one obvious theme in *Typee:* the corrupting influence of civilization on the simple, happy, carefree Polynesian natives. Melville compares the numerous virtues of the savages and their carefree way of life to the misery and corruption that are often the lot of more civilized men. At one point Tommo notes, "there seemed to be no cares, griefs, troubles, or vexations in all Typee." Again he says, "Alas for the poor savages when exposed to these polluting examples. Unsophisticated and confiding, they are easily led into every vice, and humanity weeps over the ruin then remorselessly inflicted upon them by their European civilizers."

One of the most important elements in Melville's criticism of the "rape of the islands" is his scathing attack on the missionaries, who brought a religion to the South Seas too austere for the people to understand and to accept. Tommo pleads, "Let the savages be civilized, but civilize them with benefits and not with evils; and let heathenism be destroyed, but not destroying the heathen—among islands of Polynesia, no sooner are the images overturned, the temples demolished, and the idolators converted into nominal Christians, than disease, vice, and premature death make their appearance."

Noting that the missionaries not only convert the savages to Christianity but also at the same time subjugate them to low positions even as beasts of burden, Melville tells the story of the wife of a missionary who took a daily ride in a little go-cart which was drawn by two of her converted natives. "Behold the glorious result! The abominations of Paganism have given way to the pure rites of the Christian worship; the ignorant savage has been supplanted by the refined European."

Many of the critics have felt the theme of *Typee* to be a more abstract one. It is the hero's search for the innocence and simplicity of the Garden of Eden. It is man's search, his everlasting search, for the remote—the faraway. It is a return to the hero's own childhood. It is a search for love for one who suffered from too little love. One can readily see that for a novel so rich in meaning as this one, one searches in vain for a single theme. Undoubtedly there are more than the themes and levels of meaning discussed here.

D. H. Lawrence speaks of Melville's soul "forever writhing in revolt." When he had something definite to rebel against, Melville was happy in his misery: the deplorable conditions aboard the whaling ships, the injustice and folly of missionaries, the miscarriage of justice in law and order.

STYLE

One critic has stated that the style of a novel is the man himself. If this statement is true, *Typee* is unmistakably Melville. Poetic language, profuse details, anecdotes, digression, allusions, poetic rhythms, flowing diction, puns, flashes of humor, inversions, suspense, understatement, adventure, a mixture of realism and romance, tone-coloring, picture-making, set pieces, satire, irony, and symbolism—these are obvious features of Melville's style.

The style of *Typee* reveals the usual weakness of a first novel. Frequently, however, one catches glimpses of the Melville genius destined to be fulfilled later in *Moby Dick*. In *Typee* Melville's genius is most evident in his handling of humor, humor that is salty, commonplace, and unsubtle. In the first chapter Melville relates the story of a cannibal queen who shocked the French navy on her state visit to an American ship, acting in unceremonious and unladylike fashion by expression of wild delight in the tattoos of "an old salt, whose bare arms and feet and exposed breast were covered with as many inscriptions in India ink as the lid of an Egyptian sarcophagus."

Ignoring "the sly hints and remonstrances of the French officers, the queen pulled open the bosom of the sailor's duck frock and rolled up the legs of his trousers, all the while gazing with admiration at the sights thus disclosed to view." Melville asks us to picture the embarrassment and the consternation of the polite French officers "when all at once the royal lady, eager to display the hieroglyphics on her own sweet form, bent forward a moment, and turning sharply around, threw up the skirt of her mantle, and revealed a sight from which the aghast Frenchman retreated precipitately, and tumbling into their boat, fled the scene of so shocking a catastrophe."

Although the humor of *Typee* is sometimes crude and heavy-handed, and even savage in its irony and sarcasm, at times it shows a tolerance and humaneness that makes it rare. Indeed, it is the humor in the novel that sets it far above the average travelogue.

Sometimes in the novel Melville employs what might be called mock-heroic irony by using excessively elaborate language to describe very simple things. For example, in describing the terrible food provided for the sailors aboard the *Dolly*, he writes that it has been served "for the nourishment and gastronomic enjoyment of the crew." As a matter of fact much of the irony in the novel derives from Melville's description of food.

In describing the captain's meal of the last rooster on the ship, Melville likens it to a funeral. "His attenuated body will be laid out upon the captain's table next Sunday, and long before night will be buried with all the usual ceremonies beneath the worthy individual's breast." Later he describes the way the natives prepare meat for a feast: "Such is the summary style in which the Typees convert perverse-minded and rebellious hogs into the most docile and amiable pork: a morsel of which placed on the tongue melts like a soft smile from the lips of Beauty." Even in referring to the natives' appetite for human flesh, Melville writes, "taking it into their heads to make a convivial meal of a poor devil—a more humane, gentlemanly, and amiable set of epicures do not probably exist in the Pacific."

Ironic commentary abounds in Melville's treatises on the treatment of the savages by the civilized world and the powerful man's behavior toward those dependent upon him. In the latter situation in speculating upon the captain's probable outrage that one of his best men has jumped ship, Tommo comments: "I know that our worthy captain, who felt such a paternal solicitude for the welfare of his crew, would not willingly consent that one of his best hands should encounter the perils of a sojourn among the natives of a barbarous island."

Melville is now considered one of our most imaginative and symbolic writers. Although *Typee* is relatively simple when compared to some of his later works, it is nevertheless rich in symbolism. Besides the obvious symbols of the Typee valley as a Garden of Eden, Tommo as Adam, and Fayaway as Eve, the novel abound in more subtle symbols. In another sense Tommo and Toby are the tempters and intruders in Paradise. It is for this reason that when they enter the valley Melville describes their approach as "gliding in the fashion of serpents."

When Tommo and Toby first enter the Typee valley after going without food for four days, their first thought is to avail themselves of some of the abundant fruit growing there. Sighting some almost immediately, Toby "quickly cleared one of the trees on which there were two or three of the fruit, but to our chagrin it proved to be much decayed; the rinds were partly opened by the birds and their hearts half devoured."

Tommo's leg, which will not heal in the valley, is cured and Tommo's physical strength returns once he is again aboard a whaling ship. Marnoo, whose special sanctity over others was generated by the physical and spiritual freedom of his taboo status, has been viewed as the true Promethean character.

Melville read other accounts of Polynesian life and incorporated some of these facts into his narrative. For example, in the first chapter of *Typee* Melville mentions *A Visit to the South Seas,* written by a certain Captain Stewart of an American sloop-of-war. Melville was considerably indebted to Stewart's account. Many of the passages in *Typee* correspond to a remarkable degree to similar descriptions in Stewart's work. Melville, however, used this and other sources to suit his own purposes.

When the book first appeared, the style of *Typee* was praised for its freshness and for the life and truth in the descriptions. Such terms as *easy, graceful,* and *graphic* were applied to the style. On reading the novel today one finds that the same qualities still abound. Amazingly they have stood the test of time.